SCRUM GUIDEBOOK

SCRUM STUDY GUIDE

Certified Scrum Master
Test Prep
Updated: 2019

- Practice Tests and Questions
- Techniques and Tips
- Pass the Test Guidance

GO FROM BOOK SMART TO AGILE SMART

Contributors:

Jan Beaver, PhD, CST
Senior Trainer
3Back LLC

A.J. Biddles, CSM, CSPO, CSP
Senior Consultant
3Back LLC

Dan Rawsthorne, PhD, CST
Chief Scientist
3Back LLC

Doug Shimp, CST
President
3Back LLC

Many of the designations used by manufacturers and sellers to distinguish their products are claimed as trademarks. Where these designations appear in this book and the authors were aware of a trademark claim, the designations have been printed in initial caps, all caps, or with appropriate registration symbols.

The authors have taken care in the preparation of this document, but make no expressed or implied warranty of any kind and assume no responsibility for errors or omissions. No liability is assumed for incidental or consequential damages in connection with or arising out of the use of the information contained herein.

Version 3 printed May 21, 2019

ISBN-13: 9781095293140

This Book is dedicated to:

All of the wonderful students we have had and clients that we have helped implement Scrum.

It is offered to our community of like-minded agilists, with whom we have had many discussions. Our discussions have helped build a body of knowledge around what it takes to build quality software systems.

Without whom this book could not exist.

Table of Contents

THIS PAGE INTENTIONALLY LEFT BLANK

TIP: "Address Complex Adaptive Problems"

Chapter 1: Introduction

Agile concepts have been used for decades (if not centuries) in complexity theory, war theory, project management, sociology, and most sciences. Agile practices show us how to "think about" and manage the work required for solving complicated and complex problems. The Scrum Guide says Scrum is for solving complex adaptive problems. In the last 25 years or so, agile concepts have become popular in software development, and there are several pathways you could take in order to be agile. One of these pathways is Scrum, the most popular agile software process in the world.

This study guide has two purposes. The first is to help you pass the Certified Scrum Master test. The second is to give you a deeper understanding of Scrum so that you can begin to apply it successfully to your real world needs.

Certifications are necessary because they help employers find and recognize people with specific skills; people with Certifications are more likely to "get the job".

However, Certifications do not mean that people actually have the skills to "do the job". Therefore, we are passionate about making this study guide a combination of exam knowledge and real-world knowledge of modern Scrum.

We do not differentiate between these kinds of knowledge in the main text of the guide; this guide focuses on the 2017 Scrum Guide, which is the focus of the test and the most current practices and philosophies in common use today. We have separated some specific exam knowledge (tips and tricks) into sidebars in the guide. This is necessary to point out instances when the exam wants something that is not necessarily true in the real-world, or when the exam has a specific point of view you need to understand, or something like that. These distinctions will help you understand the difference between "exam knowledge" and "real-world knowledge". The distinctions will help you decipher and pass the test quickly.

The Scrum Study Guide is not intended to give you a deep understanding of modern Scrum – this would take hundreds of pages, and thousands of hours of practice.

However, this Scrum Study Guide will help you pass the exam and, we hope, give you a better understanding of Scrum.

Please send us feedback so that we can update the Scrum Study Guide for others. info@scrumguide.com

TIP: "The Agile Manifesto was originally about software but has been applied to all domains of work."

Chapter 2: General Knowledge

Agile Manifesto

In 2001 a group of developers got together in Snowbird, Utah to talk about what they had learned about modern software development. The result was the Agile Manifesto:

Manifesto for Agile Software Development

We are uncovering better ways of developing software by doing it and helping others do it. Through this work we have come to value:

Individuals and Interactions *over* Processes and tools
Working Software *over* Comprehensive Documentation
Customer Collaboration *over* Contract Negotiation
Responding to Change *over* Following a Plan

That is, while there is value in the items on the right, we value the items on the left more.

Although agile software development processes had been around a long time, this was probably the most significant milestone in the area of software agility, as it firmly established the word "Agile" as the generic term for a wide-ranging family of tools, teams, and organizations, including Scrum.

Each of the Four Agile Manifesto Values statements is a preference that few of us would disagree with, and the Scrum Framework will help you find your own process that balances the preferences and works for you. Each of the four statements is important, but the most important is the last one.

This value statement, "Responding to Change *over* Following a Plan," is about agility, which is the concept of basing all decisions on today's reality rather than following a preconceived plan. For many people this requires a significant paradigm shift. We need to change from wanting to know what we're doing (following a plan) to figuring out what to do based on today's realities (being agile).

Twelve Principles of Agile Software

There are 12 principles that sit behind the Agile Manifesto and clarify some of the thoughts that go into being Agile:

1. Our highest priority is to satisfy the customer through early and continuous delivery of valuable software.

2. Welcome changing requirements, even late in development. Agile processes harness change for the customer's competitive advantage.

3. Deliver working software frequently, from a couple of weeks to a couple of months, with a preference to the

shorter timescale.

4. Business people and developers must work together daily throughout the project.

5. Build projects around motivated individuals. Give them the environment and support they need, and trust them to get the job done.

6. The most efficient and effective method of conveying information to and within a development team is face-to-face conversation.

7. Working software is the primary measure of progress.

8. Agile processes promote sustainable development. The sponsors, developers, and users should be able to maintain a constant pace indefinitely.

9. Continuous attention to technical excellence and good design enhances agility.

10. Simplicity – the art of maximizing the amount of work not done – is essential.

11. The best architectures, requirements, and designs emerge from self-organizing teams.

12. At regular intervals, the team reflects on how to become more effective, then tunes and adjusts its behavior accordingly.

These principles seem dogmatic, using words like "all" and "every," and this seems inconsistent with the Manifesto itself. Don't worry about it; this inconsistency is not a big deal. Just remember that it's always about balance and what's good for your team.

Exam Notes

- There are usually questions about the Manifesto. We suggest that you simply memorize it...

- An in-depth knowledge of the 12 underlying principles is not necessary. However, principle 11 shows up quite often. Just remember that architecture, design, and requirements emerge.

Scrum Foundations

Empirical versus Defined Processes

There are two major approaches to controlling any process:

- Defined Process Control, and

- Empirical Process Control.

The Defined Process Control model requires that every piece of work be completely understood (think manufacturing). Given a well-defined set of inputs, the same outputs are generated every time (i.e. make a tea kettle). A defined process can be started and allowed to run until completion, with the same results every time (make 1000 tea kettles).

The Empirical Process Control model provides and exercises control through frequent 'inspect and adapt' cycles (Two Pillars of Scrum). This is designed for processes that are imperfectly defined and generate unpredictable and unrepeatable outputs. There are three Pillars defined as essential to the original Scrum empirical process.

- <u>Transparency</u>, progress of the Development Team's work must be visible so that those outside the Team can make informed decisions and 'inspect and adapt'.

- <u>Inspection</u>, is used to assess progress towards a Sprint Goal or bigger goals.

- <u>Adaptation</u> is used to alter direction and change how we are doing it.

An empirical process is usually thought of as something with a feedback loop. Agile practitioners know that without feedback loops you will fail. Empiricism asserts that experience is the 'best teacher' and that the realities uncovered will cause you to change your plans often. Scrum relies on transparency of the work with frequent inspection that will lead to adaptation.

Sprint

A Sprint is a time-boxed event; it is a synonym for Iteration. Sprints have a maximum length of one month, and can be as short as one day; the most common lengths of Sprints are one, two, or three weeks.

TIP: the Sprint is the heart-beat of Scrum.

Sprints are used to coordinate teams together, seek meaningful feedback, and steer outcomes. The more complex the situation, the smaller and more quickly you want to iterate and get feedback thus, the shorter you want your Sprints to be.

Small quick steps can inform decision-making. Big long steps delay information and learning.

TIP: Sprint cycles help us build increments quickly for frequent inspection and adaptation.

Significance of "Done"

A Scrum Team must deliver a "Done" Increment every Sprint. What does this mean?

TIP: The Increment is one of three artifacts declared in the Scrum Guide.

There are two dimensions for the Increment: its features, and how close to releasable those features are. "Done" is about releasable. Think of it as two questions:

- Is the feature, as defined, well tested?

- Is the code well crafted (definition of "Done" – DoD)?

If we can answer "yes" to these questions, then the Increment is "Done" – if we can't, it isn't. The Development Team needs to certify that all necessary work has been done on the Increment.

Imagine that "Done" is an end point. For example, if we had a party with confetti everywhere, and we needed to clean the room, we might have some clean-up to do.

1. Initially Known Product Backlog Item: "Clean Room"

2. Refined Product Backlog Item with attributes "Description: Clean Room of Confetti, Estimate: a few hours, Value: happy customer, Order: Now, Tests: No confetti is visible and everything is picked up."

Let the team just "Get To Done" using an empirical process (a.k.a. Sprint).

TIP: The increment is the sum of all previous sprint increments plus the current one and they are all expected to work or be ready to ship. In other words it fully meets the understood definition of "Done" and quality has not decreased.

Scrum Values

The Scrum Guide has five values as originally defined in 2006 but not formally added to the Scrum Guide until 2016.

Openness	There should be no secrets between/amongst Team Members about things relevant to Production; the Team Members should be open to suggestions from others.
Focus	Everything that the Team does must have a focus; and the Team Members must focus on what is important in everything they do.
Commitment	The Team makes and keeps its commitments/agreements; and the Team Members must have commitment to the Team and the Product itself.
Respect	Team Members believe that people are always doing the best they can do at any given moment; they respect all points of view, including those of their Stakeholders.
Courage	The Team must have the courage to make reality visible, the courage to say No; and

	Team Members must have the courage to be open with each other.

Good Scrum Teams are self-organized, cross-functional and value-driven. We call such a team a Well-Formed Team (WFT). The fact that the Scrum Guide formally included Values that teams should use was a good addition, but specifying which values to include remains controversial.

TIP: You will need to know the Scrum Guide values.

TIP: The Values 'Openness' and 'Courage' are often used interchangeably. When in doubt, choose Courage.

Applicability of Scrum

TIP: Scrum is suitable for solving complex adaptive problems.

Scrum has been applied successfully to many domains. For example, Scrum has been applied to all forms of software development, medical devices, financial systems, embedded systems, marketing, construction, bridge building and just about any vertical industry that you can think of.

Exam Notes

- There are usually questions about the empirical process. Review the three pillars of the process.

- Understanding the "Definition of Done" is crucial; remember that it's about quality of the Increment, not the number of features in the Increment.

- Scrum has been successfully applied all kinds of industries.

> Anywhere humans are dealing with complex problems, Scrum can be applied.

Scrum Team

A Scrum Team is a relatively small group of people whose job is to produce valuable, high-quality products in an iterative, incremental manner. There are only three roles played by members of the Scrum Team: Scrum Master, Product Owner, and Development Team Member. There is only one Scrum Master and one Product Owner, and either or both of them may also be members of the Development Team.

TIP: The Development Team has 3-9 members; if the Scrum Master and Production Owner do development work, then they are part of the count.

The Scrum Team is cross- functional, self-organized, and "lives" the Scrum Values – each of these concepts is discussed elsewhere in this Guide.

Exam Notes

- In this guide, we explicitly use the phrases "Scrum Team" and "Development Team" (or "DevTeam") to reduce confusion.

- The CSM test also uses the word "Team" as a collective role, which could be either the Scrum Team or Development Team, based on context. Don't let this confuse you!

Scrum Master

The Scrum Master plays a role unique to Scrum, and it is hard to describe by comparing it to existing roles. Let's start by describing some of the things the Scrum Master is not. The Scrum Master is not:

- A Manager of the Scrum Team or any of its members

- The Project Manager

- Assigner of tasks to Team Members

- Responsible for making sure everyone is busy

- Evaluator the Team's work for completeness or desirability

- Responsible for the success of the product

Given all that, what does the Scrum Master do?

Simply put, the Scrum Master's job is to produce a DevTeam that can develop high-quality products at a sustainable pace.

TIP: The Scrum Master does this by being a servant-leader in service to the Product Owner, Development Team and Organization.

The Product Owner will use the Development Team to build valuable products for the organization. The Scrum Master fosters teamwork and instills in each Scrum Team member the notion that Team success trumps individual success. The Scrum Master acts as a facilitator and servant-leader and has a substantial list of responsibilities directed at creating a strong, self-organized, cross-functional Team that lives the Scrum

Values and works in an Organization that knows how to use Scrum.

Scrum Master Responsibilities

Implement the Scrum Framework

The Scrum Master is responsible for ensuring the Team understands Scrum and uses it effectively. The Scrum Master must understand the Scrum framework in sufficient breadth and depth to implement it with the Scrum Team. The Scrum Master is responsible for teaching everyone on the Scrum Team about Scrum and coaching them to perform their roles appropriately – and this includes the Product Owner!

Service to the Organization

Scrum Masters must push for changes in the Organization in support of Scrum – they must make the Organization a better place for Scrum Teams to live, work, and grow. The Scrum Masters within an organization lead and coach the Organization on its Scrum adoption, and work together to increase the effectiveness of Scrum in the Organization. Scrum Masters often let Scrum speak for itself, and "market" Scrum by simply advertising the increased effectiveness of the Team.

Service to the Product Owner and Development Team

The Scrum Master assists and serves the needs of the Development Team and Product Owner. As the servant-leader of the Scrum Team, the Scrum Master works with the Organization to ensure that Development Team members and the Product Owner have everything they need to do their jobs as effectively as possible. The Scrum Master actively facilitates communication and collaboration between the Development Team and Product Owner, and uses facilitation skills within the Development Team to foster empowerment, creativity, and self-organization.

Removing Impediments

The Scrum Master is the Scrum Team member who is most responsible for assuring impediments are removed. Impediments consist of anything keeping the Scrum Team from working at its best. Impediments come in many shapes and sizes, from minor blocking issues to major, organization-wide dysfunctions. The Scrum Master often works with the Product Owner, Development Team members, or people outside the Scrum Team to eliminate Impediments. The Scrum Master coaches the Scrum Team how to remove its own impediments as part of the Scrum Team's self- organization. The Scrum Master works with the Product Owner to assure impediment removal is prioritized appropriately.

Act as a Scrum Coach

The Scrum Master engages in continuous teaching, coaching, and mentoring of the Product Owner, Development Team members, and people outside the Scrum Team. The Scrum Master continuously works with the Team and Product Owner on strategies to improve teamwork, productivity, practices, and tools. The Scrum Master ensures the Product Owner and members of the Development Team are performing their roles effectively and working together to deliver valuable, high-quality product every Sprint. The Scrum Master helps those outside the Scrum Team understand how to work with the Scrum Team: to understand which of their interactions with the

Scrum Team are helpful and which are not.

<u>Protect the Team</u>

The Scrum Master protects the Development Team from outside interruptions or interference during the Sprint. Once the Development Team commits to a Sprint Goal, Scrum allows no interference in the Development Team's pursuit of the Sprint Goal. It is the Scrum Master's job to ensure the entire Organization (including the Product Owner, if he or she is not a member of the Development Team) respects the Development Team's absolute authority to deliver its commitment to the Sprint Goal – and to do this work at a sustainable pace. It is important that the Development Team does not commit to completing all the Items on the Sprint Backlog – it commits to the Sprint Goal. This "wiggle room" is necessary to allow the Development Team to do high-quality work and meet the appropriate Definition of Done.

<u>Guide the Team</u>

The Scrum Master guides the Team by living and demonstrating the Scrum values and principles, every day, all the time. By modeling these key values and principles, the Scrum Master leads by example, encouraging and challenging the Scrum Team – and the Organization as a whole – to follow suit and remain true to the spirit of Scrum.

Scrum Master Authority

The Scrum Master's authority is not managerial authority – it is moral authority granted by the Development Team itself. This authority is based entirely in a deep knowledge and understanding of Agile and Scrum values, principles, and practices. The Scrum Master influences the team.

The Scrum Master cannot make decisions for the Team. The Scrum Master cannot assign tasks or commit to scope or delivery dates on behalf of the Team. The Scrum Master cannot tell the Team to put more – or less – work into a Sprint. The Scrum Master cannot also serve as the Product Owner; in fact, the Scrum Master is often protecting the Development Team from the Product Owner.

Exam Notes

- For the CSM Test, it is important to remember that the Scrum Master has no managerial authority.

- For the CSM Test, it is important to remember that the Scrum Master is not interested in on-time delivery or value. He or she is only interested in helping the Team do its job better through following the Scrum rules and practices.

Product Owner

The Product Owner role is pivotal in Scrum.

TIP: The Product Owner is accountable to the organization for maximizing the value of the Development Team's work results (Product).

While the Scrum Master's job is to produce a Development Team that can develop high-quality products at a sustainable pace, the Product Owner uses the Development Team to build valuable products for the Business.

This looks something like a standard management role; it may even remind you of a Project Manager. Don't be fooled! This is a completely new role. The way a Product Owner works with the Scrum Team is much different from what most managers would do.

Team Member

The Product Owner is a full-fledged member of the Scrum Team. The Product Owner is part of the self-organized, cross-functional Scrum Team, and may be a member of the Dev Team, as well. The Product the Product Owner is accountable for is "the product that results from the Dev Team's work."

No Project Manager

Scrum does not define a role called Project Manager. The responsibilities of the project manager are split between the Product Owner, who determines what needs to be done and in what order; and the Team, which decides how much gets done and how it gets implemented. Project management occurs, but the Scrum way of dividing authority and responsibility produces a pull system that emphasizes product quality and a laser-like focus on customer and stakeholder value.

An Individual Role

TIP: The Product Owner must be an individual, not a committee or group. Scrum is absolutely adamant on this point. It comes down to decision-making and accountability: the Product Owner is the only Scrum Team Member accountable for the success of the product; therefore the Product Owner must have the authority to make key decisions to drive the Scrum Team toward success. This authority and accountability cannot be shared. The Product Owner may get help, guidance, and assistance from the Scrum Master, the Development Team, and external Stakeholders, but the Product Owner retains the accountability and authority.

Since the Product Owner is the only Scrum Team Member with the accountability and authority to make critical decisions, the person filling the Product Owner role must not have divided responsibilities within the Organization. If the Product Owner is too busy or distracted with other duties to interact appropriately with the Development Team and make necessary decisions, the success of the Scrum Team and the product is jeopardized.

Product Authority

The Product Owner's decision-making authority falls into two critical areas: the ordering of Items in the Product Backlog and deciding when the product is releasable. In these two areas, the Product Owner's authority is absolute, but the Product Owner would be foolish to ignore the advice of the Development Team. On the other hand, the Product Owner does not have authority over how the work gets done or how much work gets done every Sprint. These areas are under the Development Team's control, so the Product Owner and Development Team must work together (often using the Scrum Master as referee) to ensure the right products emerge at the right time.

In particular, the Product Owner is not allowed to demand the Development Team work faster. The Product Owner is not allowed to tell the Development Team how much work they must do in a Sprint. And the Product Owner is not allowed to demand the Definition of Done be "watered down" in order to produce more products. Making sure the Product Owner does not do these things is part of the Scrum Master's "Protect the Team" responsibility.

So, how does the Development Team work with the Product Owner? Basically, here's how it works. The Product Owner prioritizes the Product Backlog, which determines the order that Backlog Items will be worked on. The Development Team develops the Backlog Items as fast as they can, to the desired quality, while working at a sustainable pace. They do this one Sprint at a time, meeting Sprint Goals and delivering a potentially shippable Product Increment each Sprint.

During the Sprints, the Product Owner works with the Development Team to answer questions and provide guidance about the Items. At the end of each Sprint, the Product Owner, the Development Team, and Stakeholders have a Sprint Review to discuss the products and determine what to do next. By observing the velocity of production, the Product Owner can refine forecasts about when the Product will be ready for delivery.

Finally, when the Product Owner determines the Product Increment the Team has produced is ready, the Product Owner has the authority to release it.

Product Owner Responsibilities

The Product Owner's responsibilities are different from those of the Scrum Master. The Scrum Master's primary focus is the Team and the Product Owner's responsibilities are focused on developing Product and the Scrum Team's success. This is one reason why different people usually fill the Scrum Master and Product Owner roles.

Even though the Product Owner is a single person, other Scrum Team members (and even external Subject Matter Experts) may help the Product Owner with his or her responsibilities. This is a self-organization issue, and does not relieve the Product Owner from the accountability for carrying out these responsibilities. In other words, the Product Owner is accountable for getting these things done, but may have help from others to actually get them done.

Own the Product Vision

The Product Owner owns the Product Vision, which is an overarching statement that answers the question: Why are we doing this? Since the Product the Product Owner is accountable for is the one created by his or her Dev Team, it could be part of a bigger Product that is being delivered by the Organization. Therefore, the Product Vision could be part of a larger Product Vision that is owned by some sort of higher-level Product Owner.

TIP: 'Higher-level' is confusing and leads to a concept of a layering of Product Owners. Ignore this for the exam; the Scrum Guide assumes there is only one Team and one Product. The layering of Product Owners is a Scaling issue, and is outside the scope of the Scrum Guide, and thus outside the scope of the CSM Exam.

The Product Vision is typically a brief statement of purpose, and it keeps everyone focused while they do their daily work. It can take any form, from the classic "elevator pitch" to something more formal. Scrum specifies neither the format nor content of the Product Vision, but it does require that the Vision be visible to all.

Create and Maintain the Product Backlog

The Product Owner manages the Product Backlog, the list of items representing everything necessary to deliver on the Product Vision. The Product Owner usually creates the initial Product Backlog in concert with the Product Vision. The Scrum Team only has one Product Backlog, even though it may work on many different products. The Product Backlog, in this case, is a combined list showing how the Development Team will balance and interweave the development of the products – and the prioritization across the products is done by the Product Owner.

The Product Owner is responsible for maintaining the Product Backlog as it emerges. This has several facets:

TIP: First, the Product Owner updates the Product Backlog to reflect best understood and currently known requirements; the product backlog evolves.

TIP: Second, the Items on the Product Backlog need to be refined.

TIP: Third, the Product Backlog needs to be ordered so everyone understands the prioritization.

As usual, the Scrum Team may assist the Product Owner with this work, but the Product Owner is accountable to get it done.

Drive Product Success

The Product Owner aids the Scrum Team's success by providing the Team with the latest information on customer and market needs. The Product Owner is the primary interface on the Scrum Team to the world of stakeholders, customers, and the market area in which the Product lives.

Collaborate with the Team

Scrum very deliberately places the Product Owner, along with the Scrum Master and Development Team Members, into a single unit called the Scrum Team. Within the Scrum Team there is a shared Product Vision and common interest in delivering a valuable, high-quality product at a sustainable pace.

Continuous Product Owner collaboration with the Development Team is vital to the success of the Scrum Team. When Development Team members have product- related questions about the work, they refer to the Product Owner for answers. The Product Owner may not be a Subject Matter Expert (SME), but the Product Owner should know how to find answers. The Product Owner is not a conduit for all information often, external stakeholders work directly with team member to improve clarity about the work being done.

Similarly, the Development Team knows the technology and must collaborate with the Product Owner to ensure vital architecture, infrastructure, and other non- functional Items are represented appropriately in the Product Backlog.

Collaborate with Stakeholders

The Product Owner is the primary interface into the Scrum Team for the business, stakeholders, customers, and the market. This arrangement frees the Team Members to focus on developing high-quality product increments without having to worry about what they are working on or why they should be working on it. To allow the team to focus on developing the product, the Product Owner must collaborate with and facilitate communication between the various stakeholders regarding the product impacts. Only in this way can the Product Owner understand stakeholder needs well enough to order the Product Backlog appropriately.

Participate in Sprint Meetings

The Product Owner must be present and actively participating in the Sprint Planning, Sprint Review, and Sprint Retrospective meetings. If the Product Owner is also a member of the Development Team, the Product Owner must attend the Daily Scrum (Standup) just like everybody else. If the Product Owner is not a member of the Development Team, he or she may attend the Daily Scrum as an observer, just like any other Stakeholder.

Exam Notes

- The Product Owner is often overworked, and there are many ways to try to solve this problem, but the preferred thing to do first is to free the Product Owner from other responsibilities.

- There are many reasons the Product Owner and the Scrum Master must be different people; the one to remember is that:

TIP: one person being both the Product Owner and Scrum

> *Master would place too much power in the hands of one
> person, and could cause confusion.*

Development Team

The Development Team is the engine
of the Scrum Team. The Development
Team builds the products and ensures
that they meet the required quality standards (*TIP: definition of
"Done"*) and works to address stakeholder needs.

The Development Team's job, simply stated, is to build high-
quality products (Increments) at a sustainable pace. The
Development Team consists of three to nine members, and
either or both the Scrum Master and Product Owner may be
members. Development Team members have no titles; they are
all "Developers" no matter what their skill sets and expertise.
This includes the Scrum Master and Product Owner when they
are working as members of the Development Team.

*TIP: The PO and SM are part of the development team count
when they do development work.*

Development Team Responsibilities

Self-Organization

The Development Team is self-organizing; no one, not even the
Scrum Master (and particularly not the Product Owner) may tell
the Development Team how to build the Product Increment. It
is the Development Team's responsibility to determine how to
get the Increment to "Done" while conforming to any
organizational constraints.

Cross-Functional

The Development Team is cross-functional; all the skills needed to create a "Done" increment are on the Development Team.

Because of the highly collaborative nature of Scrum, it is highly recommended that the Scrum Team be collocated. In the ideal case, every Scrum Team Member is on the Scrum Team full-time, the whole Development Team is in the same room with the ScrumMaster, and the Product Owner is right next door.

Deliver an Increment of "Done"

The Development Team delivers a potentially shippable Product Increment every Sprint, which is then reviewed and analyzed to determine what to do next. A "potentially shippable" Increment is one in which all Items have met their Acceptance Criteria and the Increment meets its Definition of Done.

The key to delivering a potentially shippable Product Increment every Sprint is collaboration within the Development Team. Collaboration is the mechanism the Team uses for self-organizing and self-managing to ensure that all of the work needed to accomplish the Sprint Goal gets done. Team members swarm around difficult problems and take on whatever tasks are needed to move the Team closer to achieving the Sprint Goal and providing a "Done" Product Increment, regardless of individual specialty or preference.

Participate in All Scrum Meetings

TIP: The Development Team members are required to attend all Scrum Meetings and activities.

The Sprint Backlog and Monitor Progress

The Sprint Backlog is a subset of the Product Backlog that the Development Team pulls into a Sprint. The Sprint Backlog is the Development Team's primary tool for managing the work of the Sprint. The Development Team self-organizes to complete the Items on the Sprint Backlog.

TIP: Changes to the Sprint backlog must not endanger the Sprint Goal; Quality must not decrease.

There is no specified format for the Sprint Backlog, but the Development Team often puts the Sprint Backlog Items "on the wall" in the team room. In the spirit of self- organization, the Development Team will often track Sprint progress using charts or graphs to convey vital information in simple, visual formats, such as the Sprint Burndown.

The Sprint Backlog and Sprint progress charts enable and enhance the Team's self- organization, self-management, and collaboration and need to be updated continuously throughout the Sprint. In keeping with the Team's authority to self- organize and self-manage, it is up to the Team to determine how best to handle updating the Sprint Backlog and any progress charts.

TIP: Sprint Backlog is a formal artifact in Scrum that must support transparency

Development Teams Authority

Development Teams have full authority to do whatever is necessary to achieve the Sprint Goal and deliver a "Done" Product Increment. Some examples of Team authority in practice include:

- Calling on Subject Matter Experts (SMEs) for help with specific issues and problems.

- Escalating impediments to the Scrum Master.

- Receiving answers to questions directed at the Product Owner in a timely manner.

- Bringing in specialists from outside the Team to work on specific tasks that fall outside the skill sets of Team Members.

However, the Development Team's authority does not overlap with, or encroach upon, the authority of the Product Owner or the Organization. This means that the Development Team does not have the authority to change the Acceptance Criteria of Sprint Backlog items without the consent of the Product Owner. The Development Team does not have the authority to unilaterally change the Definition of Done for a Product Increment. The Development Team does not have the authority to ignore externally-imposed Constraints. The Development Team does not have the authority to remove Sprint Backlog Items.

However, negotiation between the Development Team and Product Owner during a Sprint is not unusual or even undesirable – often the Development Team acquires knowledge that makes changes such as those described above desirable and even necessary. On the other hand, the Development Team and Product Owner must agree to any such changes, or one role will be overstepping its bounds and infringing on the responsibilities and accountability of the other.

Exam Notes

- Development Teams are self-organizing and focused on delivering high value product.
- Development Teams are cross-functional.

TIP: Use Scrum Events with prescribed regularity to avoid the need for other meetings.

Chapter 3: Scrum Events

Sprint Planning Meeting

Each Sprint begins with a time-boxed Sprint Planning Meeting. The length of this meeting is two hours per week of Sprint; in other words, it is four hours long for a two-week Sprint, eight hours long for a one-month Sprint, and so on. The Sprint Planning meeting is facilitated by the Scrum Master and is attended by the entire Scrum Team along with any Subject Matter Experts (SMEs) who have been invited by the Scrum Team (for the sake of Sprint Planning these SMEs are considered part of the Development Team). There are two purposes of the Sprint Planning Meeting:

1. *TIP: The Development Team commits to a Sprint Goal and provides guidance on why the increment*

is being built.

2. Sprint Backlog development, consisting of refined Backlog Items with Tasks, Acceptance Criteria, and Definitions of Done.

Sprint Planning begins with the Product Owner presenting an ordered list of refined Backlog Items to the Development Team. There should be enough Items on this list to "fill" the Sprint, and they will have been previously refined as we describe later.

The purpose of Sprint Planning is to determine how many Items will "fit" in the Sprint, not to figure out what the Items mean.

TIP: The Development answers what will 'fit' into the sprint at sprint planning or during the sprint, no one else.

There are two basic patterns of Sprint Planning: the single-pass pattern, and the double-pass pattern.

Single-Pass Pattern of Sprint Planning

In the single-pass pattern, the Product Owner and the Development Team work down the list of refined Backlog Items, considering each in turn. For each Item:

- The Product Owner and Development Team discuss the Item, with the Product Owner answering any questions the Development Team may have.

- The Product Owner and Development Team agree to and finalize the Item's Acceptance Criteria and Definition of Done.

- The Development Team discusses and identifies the Tasks and Effort required to complete the Item.

- The Development Team (without undue influence from the Product Owner) determines if the Item might "fit" in the Sprint in addition to the other Items already agreed upon in the Sprint Backlog.

This process continues until the Development Team believes that the Sprint is full. Once the Development Team has agreed to the Sprint Backlog, the Product Owner and Development Team discuss and agree on a single Sprint Goal that captures what is important about the Sprint. The Sprint Goal defines the success criteria for the Sprint and provides safety and "wiggle room" to the Development Team – overall success is defined by this Goal, and not by whether they complete the Sprint Backlog. The Team typically makes the Sprint Backlog visible on a wall-sized task board.

Double-Pass Pattern of Sprint Planning

In the double-pass pattern, Sprint Planning is broken into two equal-length parts. In the first part the Product Owner moves down the list of refined Backlog Items, considering each in turn. For each Item:

- The Product Owner and Development Team discuss the Item, with the Product Owner answering any questions the Development Team may have.

- The Product Owner and Development Team agree to and finalize the Item's Test Criteria and Definition of Done.

- The Development Team (without undue influence

from the Product Owner) determines if the Item "fits" in the Sprint in addition to the other Items already agreed upon in the Sprint Backlog.

- Once the Development Team feels that the Sprint is full, the Product Owner and Development Team discuss and agree on a single Sprint Goal that captures what is important about the Sprint and the Product Owner leaves the room.

In the second part of Sprint Planning, the Development Team goes through these Items again, discussing and identifying the Tasks and Effort needed to complete them. Once they have a good understanding of the work ahead of them, they determine which of these Items will most likely "fit" in the Sprint while paying close attention to the Sprint Goal.

Once they have completed this step, the Product Owner returns and the Development Team finalizes the Sprint Plan by telling the Product Owner which Items will most likely "fit" in the Sprint; and then they finalize the Sprint Goal. As before, the Sprint Goal defines the success criteria for the Sprint and provides safety and "wiggle room" to the Development Team – overall success is defined by this Goal, and not by whether they complete the Sprint Backlog. The Team typically makes the Sprint Backlog visible on a wall-sized taskboard.

Daily Scrum (Daily Standup)

The Daily Scrum is a 15-minute time-boxed meeting of the Development Team. The Scrum Master, Product Owner, and others may attend, but are only required if they are actively working on Sprint Backlog Items. The purpose of the meeting is to ensure that Development Team members are all "on the same page" – to ensure that they are making the best possible progress towards the Sprint Goal and the Sprint Backlog. Development Team members ensure the meeting is brief, and each of them answers the following three questions with an eye on the Sprint Backlog and Sprint Goal:

- What did I do yesterday?
- What am I doing today?
- What impediments do I have?

TIP: The three questions are not absolute. The Team can use any questions or techniques they want in order to arrive at consensus.

There may be brief clarifying questions and answers during the Daily Scrum. Detailed discussions occur after the meeting, not during. Many teams meet directly following the Daily Scrum to work on issues that have come up and to do a little planning.

Sprint Review Meeting

At the end of each Sprint, there is a Sprint Review meeting to allow Key Stakeholders to review the Increment and adapt the Product Backlog.

During the Sprint Review, the Scrum Team and Stakeholders discuss what work was done in the Sprint and what might be done in the next Sprint. Things that are not actually done (don't meet their Test Criteria and/or Definition of Done) are not to be demonstrated or discussed. These discussions are often conducted and facilitated with the Scrum Team demonstrating the Increment to the Stakeholders, but it can be done in many different ways – your Team will find its own way. This should be an informal meeting and the presentation of the Product Increment is intended to elicit feedback and foster discussions about what to do next.

The Development Team and Stakeholders discuss what they have learned, with an eye to the future. They discuss what should, and should not, be part of future Sprints. Refinement of the Product Backlog can occur as part of the Sprint Review, either in response to feedback or to meet new opportunities. In any case, the main result of the Sprint Review is a better idea of what to do moving forward.

Sprint Retrospective

At the end of each Sprint there is a Sprint Retrospective, usually held immediately after the Sprint Review. The purpose of the Retrospective is for the Scrum Team Members to discuss and improve their teamwork and/or practices. The Retrospective is a time-boxed meeting whose length is 45 minutes per week of Sprint; in other words, it is 90 minutes long for a two-week Sprint, three hours long for a one-month Sprint, and so on.

The entire Scrum Team attends this meeting, facilitated by the Scrum Master. An intrinsic part of Scrum is the Scrum Team improving itself every Sprint; this is the time. The purposes of the Sprint Retrospective are to:

- Discuss the things that went well and those needing improvement, with regards to people, relationships, process, and tools.

- Determine how to do more of the things that went well.

- Determine how to improve those things needing improvement.

Scrum is difficult and things often go awry. It is tempting, when things go poorly, to adapt Scrum to your Organization. Don't do this. Usually, when things go wrong with your Scrum Team it is Scrum telling you that something is wrong with your Organization – and that is what you need to fix. Scrum makes clear the efficacy of your work management, retrospectives are a formal way to acknowledge and address shortcomings.

Backlog Refinement

Backlog Items are often large or ambiguous when they are first added to the Product Backlog. We want our Development Team to work on small, well-understood, actionable Items. Something has to happen to these Items between the time they are put on the Backlog and the time the Development Team works on them – and this something is called Backlog Refinement (or Grooming). Refinement is an activity the Development Team (along with the Product Owner, Stakeholders, and SMEs) does to make Backlog Items well-understood and ready for Sprint Planning.

Often, we recommend the whole Scrum Team is involved in Refinement activities with these activities taking approximately ten percent of the Team's time – or approximately four hours a week. There is no particular way to do this: an hour a day, two hours twice a week, one afternoon a week, as specialized

Scrum Study Guide

Refinement Items on the Backlog, whatever...just make sure it gets done. The purpose is to make sure we prepare for the next Sprint (i.e. "What are we doing in the next Sprint?").

What are these refinement activities? Well, Refining the Backlog means the Team:

- Decomposes/Extracts/Splits large Items in order to make small ones.
- Defines Acceptance Criteria and Definitions of Done for these small Items.
- (possibly) Does some preliminary design work or tasking for these Items.

What is important is that the Backlog Items are Ready for Sprint Planning when they need to be; this means that they are small enough to complete in a Sprint and that they have preliminary Acceptance Criteria and Definitions of Done.

info@scrumguide.com, http//scrumguide.com

TIP: Transparency in work provides opportunity to Inspect and Adapt.

Chapter 4: Scrum Artifacts

Product Backlog

The Product Backlog is an ordered list of items that unfolds customer and stakeholder needs and other work necessary to build and release a product as laid out in the Product Vision. The Product Backlog is emergent, constantly changing, both in the items it contains and their ordering.  Ordering or prioritization is predicated on the latest knowledge of the product, including customer and stakeholder needs. Regular Product Backlog refinement is a key aspect of Scrum.

The items forming the Product Backlog are placed in order of importance as determined by the Product Owner. The entire

Scrum Team may contribute to the maintenance and refinement of the Product Backlog; however, the Product Owner is ultimately accountable for the contents and their order. Items near the top of the Product Backlog are smaller, more detailed, and more valuable than items further down the list. Product Backlog Items can describe functional, non-functional, architectural and infrastructure elements, and risks to be mitigated or removed. As much as possible, Product Backlog Items should describe end-to-end vertical slices of functionality that deliver customer and stakeholder value.

Before Product Backlog Items can be considered ready for inclusion into a Sprint, the Team and Product Owner must collaborate to ensure that each item is both small enough to fit within the boundaries of a Sprint, and that the expectations of the Product Owner are clearly expressed through Test Criteria (What is "Done" for any given Sprint item?).

While the Product Owner is responsible for the order of items on the Product Backlog, only the Development Team is allowed to estimate how much effort the items will take. Scrum does not define a particular estimating technique, but does encourage the Development Team to estimate effort in the simplest, most consistent, and most realistic manner possible.

Exam Notes

- The ordering of the Product Backlog is often called prioritization. Expect to see either on the test.

- Product Backlog Items that are small enough to fit in a Sprint and whose Acceptance Criteria are known are called

Ready or "actionable" Items.

Product Increment and the Definition of "Done"

At the end of every Sprint, the Team delivers a potentially shippable Product Increment. The Product Owner may realize value from the investment to date in developing the product by releasing it to customers and stakeholders. This is only possible if the Team's effort results in the Increment being complete and ready to ship, if the Product Owner should decide to do so. To assure the Product Increment is "potentially shippable," the Development Team must ensure that each completed Item meets its Acceptance Criteria, and that the Increment itself meets its Definition of Done.

Each Item can have a Definition of Done, or the Product Increment can have a Definition of Done as a whole – it really doesn't matter. When we say the Increment meets its Definition of Done, we can mean it literally, or we can mean that each completed Item meets its own Definition of Done.

In either case, we must be constantly questioning whether or not the Definition of Done is "good enough" so that an Increment meeting its Definition of Done has enough quality to ship. This should be a constant source of discussion at the Scrum Team's Retrospectives; and these discussions may result in a constantly evolving Definition of "Done".

If the Product Increment doesn't meet its Definition of Done, there is unfinished work that must be completed. Any deviation from the Development Team's Definition of Done must be explicitly stated, and the unfinished work must be added to the Product Backlog and the Product Owner will prioritize it appropriately against all other product work.

Failure to meet Acceptance Criteria or Definitions of Done every Sprint causes a number of undesirable effects on the Development Team, Product, and Organization. The Development Team must complete all unfinished work, typically immediately before the product release. Such work does not add value to the product and tends to lower Team morale.

Unfinished work accumulates in the form of defects, inconsistent architecture and design, and other significant problems that undermine the Development Team's ability to predictably deliver value. The product suffers as quality issues deprive customers and stakeholders of the value they anticipated. The Organization experiences reduced value from its investment in the product. Finally, the Product Owner loses the opportunity to release the product based on the value/investment calculation.

Exam Notes

- The phrase "potentially shippable" is sometimes called "potentially releasable" – expect to see either on the Exam.

Sprint Backlog

The Sprint Backlog is the DevTeam's plan for turning the Product Backlog Items selected during the Sprint Planning meeting into a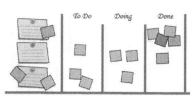
potentially shippable Product Increment. The Sprint Backlog serves two main purposes. First, it provides a detailed view into the DevTeam's expected work for the Sprint. Secondly, it is the DevTeam's primary tool for self-management of the work during the Sprint.

The DevTeam is entirely responsible for creating and maintaining the Sprint Backlog. The Sprint Backlog accurately reflects the state of each item, whether planned, in progress, or "done". Each in-progress item may indicate which DevTeam member(s) are currently working on it. The Sprint Backlog may also show the amount of effort required to complete the remaining planned and in-progress items – this information can be captured in the Sprint Burndown.

The Sprint Backlog is often implemented as a Sprint Task Board, which is a physical or tool-based depiction of the work planned, in progress, and done.

Exam Notes

- For the exam, it is important to remember that the main purpose of the Sprint Backlog is to assist the Development Team in its self-organization to get the work "done".

Burndown charts

Burndown charts illustrate the amount of work remaining, and the most common are the Sprint Burndown and the Release Burndown. The Product Owner finds

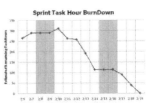

Sprint Task Hour BurnDown

the Release Burndown useful to determine when the Product might be releasable.

The Sprint Burndown chart was intended for the Team's detailed daily planning during a Sprint. Current thinking is that the Sprint Burndown Chart does more harm than good. The Sprint Burndown Chart assumes the Development Team is intending to finish everything on the Sprint Backlog. And, as we know, the Development Team's job is to complete Items as fast as they can, while meeting their Acceptance Criteria and the Product Increment's Definition of "Done", all at a sustainable pace. It is likely that focusing on finishing the list as the main priority can lead to having undone work.

TIP: Creating charts to understand progress is good however, they can't be allowed to cause quality to decrease.

Sprint Burndown Chart

The Sprint Burndown chart compares the initial estimate of work for the Sprint to the current estimate of work remaining in the Sprint. The Sprint Burndown chart is a tool for the Team to use to understand how to self-organize around the remaining Sprint work on a daily basis. The Scrum Master is responsible for making the Team aware of the current state of the Sprint Burndown chart and for encouraging the Team to keep the

Sprint Burndown chart updated every day. It is vital that the Team updates the Sprint Burndown chart daily to reflect the current status of Sprint work remaining. Without current information, the Team is not positioned to determine how to proceed with Sprint work.

Even though the Sprint Burndown is being deprecated, it is still used by many Teams. This is unfortunate.

Release Burndown Chart

The Release Burndown chart uses empirical data collected at the end of every Sprint to project the likely end date of the release, or the amount of Product Backlog that will be completed by a specified date. The data used consists of the Team's estimates of total work for the Release and the aggregate of the estimated work the Team completes each Sprint. The Release Burndown chart is updated after every Sprint with a new data point.

TIP: The Scrum Guide advocates monitoring Sprint Progress, but a specific chart is not indicated. It is up to the Product Owner to use charts that are helpful.

The Release Burndown chart is a tool utilized by the Product Owner to manage the plan for the current product Release. The Release plan is subject to change as the Team generates empirical data points every Sprint. The Product Owner is responsible for using the Team's estimates of Product Backlog Items planned for the Release, and the empirical data generated as the Team completes each Sprint, to update the Release Burndown chart.

BuildUp Charts

The BuildUp charts are rapidly emerging as a replacement for the Burndown Chart which is deprecated in "modern Scrum". BuildUp charts may be seen on 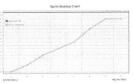 the exam, and they are so useful that we feel obligated to describe them here.

BuildUp charts are used to address reporting needs and understand Sprint progress. A BuildUp chart is built from the fundamental unit for managing a team's work: a "Story". These charts were first named and described in *Exploring Scrum: The Fundamentals*. The BuildUp Chart contains the progression of Stories being completed, and there are both Sprint and Release BuildUp charts.

Chapter 5: Test Information from Scrum Alliance

The Scrum Alliance has issued guidance about the revised CSM exam, which went into action in January 2019.

There are four distinct exams, and you will get one of them randomly. Each of them has 50 questions, and you have one hour to take it. The passing score is 37/50.

The table on the next page shows the subject areas being tested along with the 38 study areas. In the following pages we present each of the study areas along with relevant portions of the Agile Manifesto or Scrum Guide, whichever is appropriate.

In other words, this section is *guaranteed* to contain the answers to the exam. Study it and have it available during the exam. The exam is open-book, and you will do fine.

Domain Table

CSM Domains	CSM should demonstrate knowledge of ...	Number of Questions
A. Scrum and Agile	Four values of the Agile Manifesto Twelve principles of the Agile Manifesto Definition of Scrum Relationship of Scrum to Agile	3
B. Scrum Theory	Empirical process control as it relates to Scrum The 3 pillars of empirical process control and their importance How and why "incremental" is an important characteristic of Scrum How and why "iterative" is an important characteristic of Scrum Applicability of Scrum (addresses complex adaptive problems across multiple industries)	3
C. Scrum Values	Identify the five Scrum values How and why commitment is an important Scrum value How and why courage is an important Scrum value How and why focus is an important Scrum value How and why openness is an important Scrum value How and why respect is an important Scrum value	3
D. Scrum Team	Why self-organizing is an important characteristic of Scrum teams Why cross-functional is an important characteristic of Scrum teams Identify the roles on the Scrum team Identify the responsibilities and characteristics of the ScrumMaster Identify the responsibilities and characteristics of the Scrum Product Owner Identify the responsibilities and characteristics of the Scrum Development Team	10
E. Scrum Master	Understanding responsibilities and characteristics of the ScrumMaster -- servant leader for the Scrum team ScrumMaster service to the Organization -- coaching, facilitation, removing impediments ScrumMaster service to the Development Team -- coaching, facilitation, removing impediments ScrumMaster service to the Product Owner -- coaching, facilitation, removing impediments	11
F. Scrum Events	Characteristics, value and/or purpose of the Sprint Sprint planning -- characteristics, value, purpose and/or role of participants Daily Scrum -- characteristics, value, purpose and/or role of participants Sprint review -- characteristics, value, purpose and/or role of participants Retrospective -- characteristics, value, purpose and/or role of participants	10
G. Scrum Artifacts	Understand the purpose and value of Scrum artifacts Identify Scrum artifacts Product backlog - characteristics, value and purpose Sprint backlog -- characteristics, value and purpose Increment -- characteristics, value and purpose Understanding importance of transparency of artifacts to evaluate value and risk Identify the downsides of lack of transparency Importance of establishing the Definition of Done Characteristics of Product Backlog items	10

In the following pages we present each of the study areas along with relevant portions of the Agile Manifesto or Scrum Guide, whichever is appropriate.

Scrum and Agile

Four values of the Agile Manifesto	
	Individuals and interactions over processes and tools
	Working software over comprehensive documentation
	Customer collaboration over contract negotiation
	Responding to change over following a plan
Twelve principles of the Agile Manifesto	
	1. Our highest priority is to satisfy the customer through early and continuous delivery of valuable software.
	2. Welcome changing requirements, even late in development. Agile processes harness change for the customer's competitive advantage.
	3. Deliver working software frequently, from a couple of weeks to a couple of months, with a preference to the shorter timescale.
	4. Business people and developers must work together daily throughout the project.
	5. Build projects around motivated individuals. Give them the environment and support they need, and trust them to get the job done.
	6. The most efficient and effective method of conveying information to and within a development team is face-to-face conversation.
	7. Working software is the primary measure of progress.
	8. Agile processes promote sustainable development. The sponsors, developers, and users should be able to maintain a constant pace indefinitely.
	9. Continuous attention to technical excellence and good design enhances agility.

	10. Simplicity--the art of maximizing the amount of work not done--is essential.
	11. The best architectures, requirements, and designs emerge from self-organizing teams.
	12. At regular intervals, the team reflects on how to become more effective, then tunes and adjusts its behavior accordingly.
Definition of Scrum	
	Scrum (n): A framework within which people can address complex adaptive problems, while productively and creatively delivering products of the highest possible value. Scrum is: • Lightweight • Simple to understand • Difficult to master
Relationship of Scrum to Agile	
	Scrum is one of many Agile Processes/Frameworks. Agile is a concept, Scrum is an example. Other Agile Processes/Frameworks include eXtreme Programming (XP), DSDM, Crystal, Feature Driven Development, Agile2, Kanban, and others...

Scrum Theory

Empirical process control as it relates to Scrum	
	Scrum is founded on empirical process control theory, or empiricism. Empiricism asserts that knowledge comes from experience and making decisions based on what is known. Scrum employs an iterative, incremental approach to optimize predictability and control risk. Large Development Teams generate too much

	complexity for an empirical process to be useful. Various projective practices upon trending have been used to forecast progress, like burn-downs, burn-ups, or cumulative flows. These have proven useful. However, these do not replace the importance of empiricism. In complex environments, what will happen is unknown. Only what has already happened may be used for forward-looking decision-making. An increment is a body of inspectable, done work that supports empiricism at the end of the Sprint.
The 3 pillars of empirical process control and their importance	
	Transparency: Significant aspects of the process must be visible to those responsible for the outcome. Transparency requires those aspects be defined by a common standard so observers share a common understanding of what is being seen.
	Inspection: Scrum users must frequently inspect Scrum artifacts and progress toward a Sprint Goal to detect undesirable variances. Their inspection should not be so frequent that inspection gets in the way of the work. Inspections are most beneficial when diligently performed by skilled inspectors at the point of work.
	Adaptation: If an inspector determines that one or more aspects of a process deviate outside acceptable limits, and that the resulting product will be unacceptable, the process or the material being processed must be adjusted. An adjustment must be made as soon as possible to minimize further deviation.

How and why "incremental" is an important characteristic of Scrum	
	incremental means building a piece at a time. The increments get inspected as part of feedback. Scrum is about the feedback loop, inspecting the current increment every time...
How and why "iterative" is an important characteristic of Scrum	
	Iterative means doing the same process over and over. The process of scrum is about feedback and replanning. Scrum is about the feedback loop, inspecting the current increment every time...
Applicability of Scrum (addresses complex adaptative problems across multiple industries)	
	Scrum has been used to develop software, hardware, embedded software, networks of interacting function, autonomous vehicles, schools, government, marketing, managing the operation of organizations and almost everything we use in our daily lives, as individuals and societies.
	As technology, market, and environmental complexities and their interactions have rapidly increased, Scrum's utility in dealing with complexity is proven daily.
	Scrum proved especially effective in iterative and incremental knowledge transfer. Scrum is now widely used for products, services, and the management of the parent organization.

Scrum Values

Identify the five Scrum values	
	commitment, courage, focus, openness and respect
How and why commitment is an important Scrum value	
	People personally commit to achieving the goals of the Scrum Team.
How and why courage is an important Scrum value	
	The Scrum Team members have courage to do the right thing and work on tough problems.
How and why focus is an important Scrum value	
	Everyone focuses on the work of the Sprint and the goals of the Scrum Team.
How and why openness is an important Scrum value	
	The Scrum Team and its stakeholders agree to be open about all the work and the challenges with performing the work.
How and why respect is an important Scrum value	
	Scrum Team members respect each other to be capable, independent people.

Scrum Team

Why self-organizing is an important characteristic of Scrum teams	
	Self-organizing teams choose how best to accomplish their work, rather than being directed by others outside the team.
Why cross-functional is an important characteristic of Scrum teams	
	Cross-functional teams have all competencies needed to accomplish the work without depending on others

Scrum Study Guide

	not part of the team.
Identify the roles on the Scrum team	
	The Scrum Team consists of a Product Owner, the Development Team, and a Scrum Master.
Identify the responsibilities and characteristics of the Scrum Master	
	The Scrum Master is responsible for promoting and supporting Scrum as defined in the Scrum Guide. Scrum Masters do this by helping everyone understand Scrum theory, practices, rules, and values.
	The Scrum Master is a servant-leader for the Scrum Team. The Scrum Master helps those outside the Scrum Team understand which of their interactions with the Scrum Team are helpful and which aren't. The Scrum Master helps everyone change these interactions to maximize the value created by the Scrum Team.
Identify the responsibilities and characteristics of the Scrum Product Owner	
	The Product Owner is responsible for maximizing the value of the product resulting from work of the Development Team. How this is done may vary widely across organizations, Scrum Teams, and individuals.
	The Product Owner is the sole person responsible for managing the Product Backlog. Product Backlog management includes: • Clearly expressing Product Backlog items; • Ordering the items in the Product Backlog to best achieve goals and missions;

	• Optimizing the value of the work the Development Team performs; • Ensuring that the Product Backlog is visible, transparent, and clear to all, and shows what the Scrum Team will work on next; and, • Ensuring the Development Team understands items in the Product Backlog to the level needed. The Product Owner may do the above work, or have the Development Team do it. However, the Product Owner remains accountable.
Identify the responsibilities and characteristics of the Scrum Development Team	
	The Development Team consists of professionals who do the work of delivering a potentially releasable Increment of "Done" product at the end of each Sprint. A "Done" increment is required at the Sprint Review. Only members of the Development Team create the Increment. Development Teams are structured and empowered by the organization to organize and manage their own work. The resulting synergy optimizes the Development Team's overall efficiency and effectiveness. Development Teams have the following characteristics: • They are self-organizing. No one (not even the Scrum Master) tells the Development Team how to turn Product Backlog into Increments of potentially releasable functionality; • Development Teams are cross-functional, with all the skills as a team necessary to create a product

	Increment; • Scrum recognizes no titles for Development Team members, regardless of the work being performed by the person; • Scrum recognizes no sub-teams in the Development Team, regardless of domains that need to be addressed like testing, architecture, operations, or business analysis; and, • Individual Development Team members may have specialized skills and areas of focus, but accountability belongs to the Development Team as a whole.

Scrum Master

Understanding responsibilities and characteristics of the ScrumMaster -- servant leader for the scrum Team	
	The Scrum Master is responsible for promoting and supporting Scrum as defined in the Scrum Guide. Scrum Masters do this by helping everyone understand Scrum theory, practices, rules, and values. The Scrum Master is a servant-leader for the Scrum Team. The Scrum Master helps those outside the Scrum Team understand which of their interactions with the Scrum Team are helpful and which aren't. The Scrum Master helps everyone change these interactions to maximize the value created by the Scrum Team.
ScrumMaster service to the Organization -- coaching, facilitation, removing impediments	

	The Scrum Master serves the organization in several ways, including: • Leading and coaching the organization in its Scrum adoption; • Planning Scrum implementations within the organization; • Helping employees and stakeholders understand and enact Scrum and empirical product development; • Causing change that increases the productivity of the Scrum Team; and, • Working with other Scrum Masters to increase the effectiveness of the application of Scrum in the organization.
ScrumMaster service to the Development Team -- coaching, facilitation, removing impediments	
	The Scrum Master serves the Development Team in several ways, including: • Coaching the Development Team in self-organization and cross-functionality; • Helping the Development Team to create high-value products; • Removing impediments to the Development Team's progress; • Facilitating Scrum events as requested or needed; and, • Coaching the Development Team in organizational environments in which Scrum is not yet fully adopted and understood.

ScrumMaster service to the Product Owner -- coaching, facilitation, removing impediments	
	The Scrum Master serves the Product Owner in several ways, including: • Ensuring that goals, scope, and product domain are understood by everyone on the Scrum Team as well as possible; • Finding techniques for effective Product Backlog management; • Helping the Scrum Team understand the need for clear and concise Product Backlog items; • Understanding product planning in an empirical environment; • Ensuring the Product Owner knows how to arrange the Product Backlog to maximize value; • Understanding and practicing agility; and, • Facilitating Scrum events as requested or needed.

Scrum Events

Characteristics, value and/or purpose of the Sprint	
	The heart of Scrum is a Sprint, a time-box of one month or less during which a "Done", useable, and potentially releasable product Increment is created. Sprints have consistent durations throughout a development effort. A new Sprint starts immediately after the conclusion of the previous Sprint. Sprints contain and consist of the Sprint Planning, Daily Scrums, the development work, the Sprint Review, and the Sprint Retrospective. During the Sprint: • No changes are made that would endanger

	the Sprint Goal;
	• Quality goals do not decrease; and,
	• Scope may be clarified and re-negotiated between the Product Owner and Development Team as more is learned.
	Each Sprint may be considered a project with no more than a one-month horizon. Like projects, Sprints are used to accomplish something. Each Sprint has a goal of what is to be built, a design and flexible plan that will guide building it, the work, and the resultant product increment.
	Sprints are limited to one calendar month. When a Sprint's horizon is too long the definition of what is being built may change, complexity may rise, and risk may increase. Sprints enable predictability by ensuring inspection and adaptation of progress toward a Sprint Goal at least every calendar month. Sprints also limit risk to one calendar month of cost.
Sprint planning -- characteristics, value, purpose and/or role of participants	
	The work to be performed in the Sprint is planned at the Sprint Planning. This plan is created by the collaborative work of the entire Scrum Team.
	Sprint Planning is time-boxed to a maximum of eight hours for a one-month Sprint. For shorter Sprints, the event is usually shorter. The Scrum Master ensures that the event takes place and that attendants understand its purpose. The Scrum Master teaches the Scrum Team to keep it

within the time-box.

Sprint Planning answers the following:
  • What can be delivered in the Increment resulting from the upcoming Sprint?
  • How will the work needed to deliver the Increment be achieved?

Planning Topic One: What can be done this Sprint?

The Development Team works to forecast the functionality that will be developed during the Sprint. The Product Owner discusses the objective that the Sprint should achieve and the Product Backlog items that, if completed in the Sprint, would achieve the Sprint Goal. The entire Scrum Team collaborates on understanding the work of the Sprint.

The input to this meeting is the Product Backlog, the latest product Increment, projected capacity of the Development Team during the Sprint, and past performance of the Development Team. The number of items selected from the Product Backlog for the Sprint is solely up to the Development Team. Only the Development Team can assess what it can accomplish over the upcoming Sprint.

During Sprint Planning the Scrum Team also crafts a Sprint Goal. The Sprint Goal is an objective that will be met within the Sprint through the implementation of the Product Backlog, and it provides guidance to the Development Team on why it is building the Increment.

Planning Topic Two: How will the chosen work get done?	
	Having set the Sprint Goal and selected the Product Backlog items for the Sprint, the Development Team decides how it will build this functionality into a "Done" product Increment during the Sprint. The Product Backlog items selected for this Sprint plus the plan for delivering them is called the Sprint Backlog.
	The Development Team usually starts by designing the system and the work needed to convert the Product Backlog into a working product Increment. Work may be of varying size, or estimated effort. However, enough work is planned during Sprint Planning for the Development Team to forecast what it believes it can do in the upcoming Sprint. Work planned for the first days of the Sprint by the Development Team is decomposed by the end of this meeting, often to units of one day or less. The Development Team self-organizes to undertake the work in the Sprint Backlog, both during Sprint Planning and as needed throughout the Sprint.
	The Product Owner can help to clarify the selected Product Backlog items and make trade-offs. If the Development Team determines it has too much or too little work, it may renegotiate the selected Product Backlog items with the Product Owner. The Development Team may also invite other people to attend to provide technical or domain advice.
	By the end of the Sprint Planning, the Development Team should be able to explain to the Product Owner and Scrum Master how it intends to work as a self-organizing team to

	accomplish the Sprint Goal and create the anticipated Increment.
Daily Scrum -- characteristics, value, purpose and/or role of participants	
	The Daily Scrum is a 15-minute time-boxed event for the Development Team. The Daily Scrum is held every day of the Sprint. At it, the Development Team plans work for the next 24 hours. This optimizes team collaboration and performance by inspecting the work since the last Daily Scrum and forecasting upcoming Sprint work. The Daily Scrum is held at the same time and place each day to reduce complexity. The Development Team uses the Daily Scrum to inspect progress toward the Sprint Goal and to inspect how progress is trending toward completing the work in the Sprint Backlog. The Daily Scrum optimizes the probability that the Development Team will meet the Sprint Goal. Every day, the Development Team should understand how it intends to work together as a self-organizing team to accomplish the Sprint Goal and create the anticipated Increment by the end of the Sprint. The structure of the meeting is set by the Development Team and can be conducted in different ways if it focuses on progress toward the Sprint Goal. Some Development Teams will use questions, some will be more discussion based. Here is an example of what might be used: • What did I do yesterday that helped the Development Team meet the Sprint Goal?

• What will I do today to help the Development Team meet the Sprint Goal?

• Do I see any impediment that prevents me or the Development Team from meeting the Sprint Goal?

The Development Team or team members often meet immediately after the Daily Scrum for detailed discussions, or to adapt, or replan, the rest of the Sprint's work.

The Scrum Master ensures that the Development Team has the meeting, but the Development Team is responsible for conducting the Daily Scrum. The Scrum Master teaches the Development Team to keep the Daily Scrum within the 15-minute time-box.

The Daily Scrum is an internal meeting for the Development Team. If others are present, the Scrum Master ensures that they do not disrupt the meeting.

Daily Scrums improve communications, eliminate other meetings, identify impediments to development for removal, highlight and promote quick decision-making, and improve the Development Team's level of knowledge. This is a key inspect and adapt meeting.

Sprint review -- characteristics, value, purpose and/or role of participants	
	A Sprint Review is held at the end of the Sprint to inspect the Increment and adapt the Product Backlog if needed. During the Sprint Review, the Scrum Team and stakeholders collaborate about what was done in the Sprint. Based on that and any changes to the Product Backlog during the Sprint, attendees collaborate on the next things that could be done to optimize value. This is an informal meeting, not a status meeting, and the presentation of the Increment is intended to elicit feedback and foster collaboration. This is at most a four-hour meeting for one-month Sprints. For shorter Sprints, the event is usually shorter. The Scrum Master ensures that the event takes place and that attendees understand its purpose. The Scrum Master teaches everyone involved to keep it within the time-box. The Sprint Review includes the following elements: • Attendees include the Scrum Team and key stakeholders invited by the Product Owner; • The Product Owner explains what Product Backlog items have been "Done" and what has not been "Done"; • The Development Team discusses what went well during the Sprint, what problems it ran into, and how those problems were solved; • The Development Team demonstrates the work that it has "Done" and answers questions

about the Increment;

• The Product Owner discusses the Product Backlog as it stands. He or she projects likely target and delivery dates based on progress to date (if needed);

• The entire group collaborates on what to do next, so that the Sprint Review provides valuable input to subsequent Sprint Planning;

• Review of how the marketplace or potential use of the product might have changed what is the most valuable thing to do next; and,

• Review of the timeline, budget, potential capabilities, and marketplace for the next anticipated releases of functionality or capability of the product.

The result of the Sprint Review is a revised Product Backlog that defines the probable Product Backlog items for the next Sprint. The Product Backlog may also be adjusted overall to meet new opportunities.

Retrospective -- characteristics, value, purpose and/or role of participants

The Sprint Retrospective is an opportunity for the Scrum Team to inspect itself and create a plan for improvements to be enacted during the next Sprint.

The Sprint Retrospective occurs after the Sprint Review and prior to the next Sprint Planning. This is at most a three-hour meeting for one-month Sprints. For shorter Sprints, the event is usually shorter. The Scrum Master ensures that the event takes place and that attendants understand its purpose.

The Scrum Master ensures that the meeting is positive and productive. The Scrum Master teaches all to keep it within the time-box. The Scrum Master participates as a peer team member in the meeting from the accountability over the Scrum process.

The purpose of the Sprint Retrospective is to:
 • Inspect how the last Sprint went with regards to people, relationships, process, and tools;
 • Identify and order the major items that went well and potential improvements; and,
 • Create a plan for implementing improvements to the way the Scrum Team does its work.

The Scrum Master encourages the Scrum Team to improve, within the Scrum process framework, its development process and practices to make it more effective and enjoyable for the next Sprint.

| | During each Sprint Retrospective, the Scrum Team plans ways to increase product quality by improving work processes or adapting the definition of "Done", if appropriate and not in conflict with product or organizational standards. |
| | By the end of the Sprint Retrospective, the Scrum Team should have identified improvements that it will implement in the next Sprint. Implementing these improvements in the next Sprint is the adaptation to the inspection of the Scrum Team itself. Although improvements may be implemented at any time, the Sprint Retrospective provides a formal opportunity to focus on inspection and adaptation. |

Scrum Artifacts

Understand the purpose and value of Scrum artifacts	
	Scrum's artifacts represent work or value to provide transparency and opportunities for inspection and adaptation. Artifacts defined by Scrum are specifically designed to maximize transparency of key information so that everybody has the same understanding of the artifact.
Identify Scrum artifacts	
	Product Backlog, Sprint Backlog, Increment

Product backlog -- characteristics, value and purpose
The Product Backlog is an ordered list of everything that is known to be needed in the product. It is the single source of requirements for any changes to be made to the product. The Product Owner is responsible for the Product Backlog, including its content, availability, and ordering. A Product Backlog is never complete. The earliest development of it lays out the initially known and best-understood requirements. The Product Backlog evolves as the product and the environment in which it will be used evolves. The Product Backlog is dynamic; it constantly changes to identify what the product needs to be appropriate, competitive, and useful. If a product exists, its Product Backlog also exists. The Product Backlog lists all features, functions, requirements, enhancements, and fixes that constitute the changes to be made to the product in future releases. Product Backlog items have the attributes of a description, order, estimate, and value. Product Backlog items often include test descriptions that will prove its completeness when "Done." As a product is used and gains value, and the marketplace provides feedback, the Product Backlog becomes a larger and more exhaustive list. Requirements never stop changing, so a Product Backlog is a living artifact. Changes in business requirements, market conditions, or technology may cause changes in the Product Backlog.

Multiple Scrum Teams often work together on the same product. One Product Backlog is used to describe the upcoming work on the product. A Product Backlog attribute that groups items may then be employed.

Product Backlog refinement is the act of adding detail, estimates, and order to items in the Product Backlog. This is an ongoing process in which the Product Owner and the Development Team collaborate on the details of Product Backlog items. During Product Backlog refinement, items are reviewed and revised. The Scrum Team decides how and when refinement is done. Refinement usually consumes no more than 10% of the capacity of the Development Team. However, Product Backlog items can be updated at any time by the Product Owner or at the Product Owner's discretion.

Higher ordered Product Backlog items are usually clearer and more detailed than lower ordered ones. More precise estimates are made based on the greater clarity and increased detail; the lower the order, the less detail. Product Backlog items that will occupy the Development Team for the upcoming Sprint are refined so that any one item can reasonably be "Done" within the Sprint time-box. Product Backlog items that can be "Done" by the Development Team within one Sprint are deemed "Ready" for selection in a Sprint Planning. Product Backlog items usually acquire this degree of transparency through the above described refining activities.

Scrum Study Guide

	The Development Team is responsible for all estimates. The Product Owner may influence the Development Team by helping it understand and select trade-offs, but the people who will perform the work make the final estimate.
Sprint backlog -- characteristics, value and purpose	
	The Sprint Backlog is the set of Product Backlog items selected for the Sprint, plus a plan for delivering the product Increment and realizing the Sprint Goal. The Sprint Backlog is a forecast by the Development Team about what functionality will be in the next Increment and the work needed to deliver that functionality into a "Done" Increment.
	The Sprint Backlog makes visible all the work that the Development Team identifies as necessary to meet the Sprint Goal. To ensure continuous improvement, it includes at least one high priority process improvement identified in the previous Retrospective meeting.
	The Sprint Backlog is a plan with enough detail that changes in progress can be understood in the Daily Scrum. The Development Team modifies the Sprint Backlog throughout the Sprint, and the Sprint Backlog emerges during the Sprint. This emergence occurs as the Development Team works through the plan and learns more about the work needed to achieve the Sprint Goal.
	As new work is required, the Development Team adds it to the Sprint Backlog. As work is performed or completed, the estimated remaining work is updated.

	When elements of the plan are deemed unnecessary, they are removed. Only the Development Team can change its Sprint Backlog during a Sprint. The Sprint Backlog is a highly visible, real-time picture of the work that the Development Team plans to accomplish during the Sprint, and it belongs solely to the Development Team.
Increment -- characteristics, value and purpose	
	The Increment is the sum of all the Product Backlog items completed during a Sprint and the value of the increments of all previous Sprints. At the end of a Sprint, the new Increment must be "Done," which means it must be in useable condition and meet the Scrum Team's definition of "Done." An increment is a body of inspectable, done work that supports empiricism at the end of the Sprint. The increment is a step toward a vision or goal. The increment must be in useable condition regardless of whether the Product Owner decides to release it.
Understanding importance of transparency of artifacts to evaluate value and risk	
	Scrum relies on transparency. Decisions to optimize value and control risk are made based on the perceived state of the artifacts. To the extent that transparency is complete, these decisions have a sound basis. To the extent that the artifacts are incompletely transparent, these decisions can be flawed, value may diminish and risk may increase.

The Scrum Master must work with the Product Owner, Development Team, and other involved parties to understand if the artifacts are completely transparent. There are practices for coping with incomplete transparency; the Scrum Master must |

	help everyone apply the most appropriate practices in the absence of complete transparency. A Scrum Master can detect incomplete transparency by inspecting the artifacts, sensing patterns, listening closely to what is being said, and detecting differences between expected and real results. The Scrum Master's job is to work with the Scrum Team and the organization to increase the transparency of the artifacts. This work usually involves learning, convincing, and change. Transparency doesn't occur overnight, but is a path.
Identify the downsides of lack of transparency	
	Decisions to optimize value and control risk are made based on the perceived state of the artifacts. To the extent that transparency is complete, these decisions have a sound basis. To the extent that the artifacts are incompletely transparent, these decisions can be flawed, value may diminish and risk may increase.
Importance of establishing the Definition of Done	
	When a Product Backlog item or an Increment is described as "Done", everyone must understand what "Done" means. Although this may vary significantly per Scrum Team, members must have a shared understanding of what it means for work to be complete, to ensure transparency. This is the definition of "Done" for the Scrum Team and is used to assess when work is complete on the product Increment. The same definition guides the Development Team in knowing how many Product Backlog items it can select during a Sprint Planning. The purpose of each Sprint is to deliver Increments of potentially

releasable functionality that adhere to the Scrum Team's current definition of "Done."

Development Teams deliver an Increment of product functionality every Sprint. This Increment is useable, so a Product Owner may choose to immediately release it. If the definition of "Done" for an increment is part of the conventions, standards or guidelines of the development organization, all Scrum Teams must follow it as a minimum.

If "Done" for an increment is not a convention of the development organization, the Development Team of the Scrum Team must define a definition of "Done" appropriate for the product. If there are multiple Scrum Teams working on the system or product release, the Development Teams on all the Scrum Teams must mutually define the definition of "Done."

Each Increment is additive to all prior Increments and thoroughly tested, ensuring that all Increments work together.

As Scrum Teams mature, it is expected that their definitions of "Done" will expand to include more stringent criteria for higher quality. New definitions, as used, may uncover work to be done in previously "Done" increments. Any one product or system should have a definition of "Done" that is a standard for any work done on it.

Characteristics of Product Backlog items

Product Backlog items have the attributes of a description, order, estimate, and value. Product Backlog items often include test descriptions that will prove its completeness when "Done."

During Product Backlog refinement, items are reviewed and revised.

Higher ordered Product Backlog items are usually clearer and more detailed than lower ordered ones. More precise estimates are made based on the greater clarity and increased detail; the lower the order, the less detail. Product Backlog items that will occupy the Development Team for the upcoming Sprint are refined so that any one item can reasonably be "Done" within the Sprint time-box. Product Backlog items that can be "Done" by the Development Team within one Sprint are deemed "Ready" for selection in a Sprint Planning. Product Backlog items usually acquire this degree of transparency through the above described refining activities.

Practice Exam #1

Choose the best answer to the following questions. The answers, as well as the rationale behind them, are provided after the exam.

1. What does the Product Owner do during the Sprint Planning meeting?
    A. Makes sure the Development Team is taking enough work items to get the project done on time.
    B. Identifies items in priority order that she would like the Development Team to accomplish in the Sprint.
    C. Assigns stories and tasks to Development Team Members.
    D. Determines the length of the Sprint based on the number of items to be delivered.

2. What does the Development Team do during the first Sprint?
    A. Creates detailed designs documents for the project.
    B. All of the analysis work for the next two Sprints.
    C. Determine the rotation schedule of who will be the Scrum Master during each of the Sprints.
    D. Achieve the agreed upon Sprint Goal.

3. Should the Product Owner attend the Daily Standup, and if so, why?
    A. No, the Daily Standup is for the Development Team, and the Product Owner is not allowed to attend.
    B. Yes, the Product Owner needs to instruct the Development Team on which tasks to work on.
    C. Yes, if the Product Owner is involved in doing development team work.
    D. Yes, the Product Owner should make sure all Team Members are attending the Daily Standup.

4. Scrum is best applied to which type of work?
   A. Simple work of a routine nature
   B. Complicated problems
   C. Complex adaptive problems
   D. Repeatable

5. In Scrum, which role is responsible for assigning new members to a Scrum Team?
   A. This is outside the scope of the Scrum framework.
   B. The Scrum Master
   C. The Product Owner
   D. The Development Team

6. What is the recommended maximum Sprint length?
   A. 2 weeks
   B. one month or less
   C. 2 months
   D. There is no recommended maximum; it is up to the team to decide.

7. What does the Agile Manifesto say about planning?
   A. All planning is removed in favor of tight feedback loops.
   B. All planning must   be completed and agreed to by the business before development can begin.
   C. We value responding to change over following a plan.
   D. Planning occurs during the first half of every Sprint.

8. When should the Sprint Burndown Chart be updated?
   A. Not a formal Sprint Artifact
   B. After every day
   C. After every week
   D. After every Sprint

9. What is the purpose of the Product Backlog?
    A. For the Development Team to manage the work in the current Sprint.
    B. For the Product Owner to collect Product Backlog Items (PBIs) for the product.
    C. For the Product Owner to manage the number of hours spent on the project.
    D. For the Scrum Master to measure progress of the current Sprint.

10. Which role is primarily responsible for making decisions of scope versus schedule?
    A. The Product Owner
    B. The Scrum Master
    C. The Development Team
    D. This is outside the scope of the Scrum framework.

11. When does a Sprint end?
    A. When the Development Team has completed all its Tasks.
    B. When the Development Team has completed all its Stories.
    C. When the Development Team thinks the work is releasable.
    D. When the Sprint timebox expires.

12. Which role is primarily responsible for ensuring that the agreed upon process is followed?
    A. The Development Team
    B. The Scrum Master
    C. The Product Owner
    D. The Business Owner

13. Who guides the Team during a Sprint
    A. The Team is self-organizing and product-focused.
    B. The Scrum Master by assigning tasks during the Daily Standup.
    C. The Product Owner ensures the team is working by performing spot checks on the Team.
    D. The documentation for the product should be sufficiently detailed that it can serve as a guide.

14. Who attends the Sprint Planning meeting?
    A. The Team
    B. The Scrum Master
    C. The Product Owner
    D. All of the above

15. What is the purpose of the Sprint Review meeting?
    A. For the Development Team to show the Product Owner what they accomplished during the Sprint.
    B. For the Scrum Master to address the process.
    C. For the Stakeholders to review the product and provide feedback.
    D. To allow time for the QA team to test the work from the Sprint.

16. Who is most likely to bring up impediments during the Daily Standup?
    A. The Scrum Master
    B. The Product Owner
    C. The Development Team
    D. The Business Owner

17. Which role is responsible for maintaining the Product Backlog?
    A. The Scrum Master
    B. The Product Owner
    C. The Development Team
    D. The Business Owner

18. In a four week Sprint, how long should the Sprint Review meeting be?
    A. 2 hours.
    B. At most 4 hours.
    C. At least 8 hours.
    D. As long as necessary to obtain meaningful feedback.

19. What does the Agile Manifesto say about architecture?
    A. Architecture should be defined as part of the Product Vision.
    B. Architecture is the responsibility of the Scrum Master.
    C. The best architectures, requirements and designs emerge from self-organizing teams.
    D. Architecture is not important in an Agile project.

20. What does the Product Owner do during the Sprint?
    A. Guides the team on what to do next.
    B. Makes herself available to answer questions and provide clarifications.
    C. Manages the number of hours spent on Tasks.
    D. Makes sure the Scrum Master is applying the process.

21. What is a highly desirable quality of a good development team?
    A. It performs Tasks in the order specified by the Scrum Master.
    B. Each Team Member has a specialized skill.
    C. Each Team Member takes a turn performing the role of Scrum Master.
    D. It is self-organizing.

22. When should the progress towards goals be updated?
    A. After every day.
    B. After every week.
    C. At least every Sprint.
    D. After every Release.

23. What are the three pillars that uphold the empirical process of Scrum?
    A. Honesty, integrity, mutual respect.
    B. Planning, execution, release.
    C. Transparency, inspection, adaptation.
    D. Self-organized, product-focused, driven.

24. Which role is responsible for the business value of the product delivered?
    A. The Scrum Master
    B. The Product Owner
    C. The Team
    D. The Stakeholders

25. Scrum has a definition of "Done", what does this help a Team produce?
    A. An increment of functionality ready for testing.
    B. An increment of potentially shippable product.
    C. A complete use case document.
    D. An accurate release schedule.

Practice Exam #1 (Answers)

Use this answer sheet to check your answers on the Practice Test.

1. What does the Product Owner do during the Sprint Planning meeting?

B) Identifies stories in priority order that she would like the Team to accomplish during the Sprint.

The Product Owner's main responsibility is to tell the team "what's next." The Stories are identified in priority order and it is up to the Team to determine whether or not the Story (and its Done criteria) is well understood and can fit in the Sprint.

2. What does the Team do during the first Sprint?

D) Achieve the agreed upon Sprint Goal.

Many times the Startup Sprint (or Sprint Zero, Inception Sprint, etc...) is used to set up the Team to get ready to do work in the subsequent Sprints (i.e., "priming the pump," "preparing the ground," etc.), but this is not always the case. Regardless, the Team should always be working to achieve the Sprint Goal during every Sprint, including the first Sprint.

3. Should the Product Owner attend the Daily Standup, and if so, why?

C) Yes, if the Product Owner is involved in doing development team work.

Scrum does not require the Product Owner to attend the Daily Standup unless he/she is doing Development Work, but it is in the interest of the Development Team and the product for the Product Owner to attend. The Daily Scrum is for the

Development Team members to self-organize and meet Sprint Goal.

4. Scrum is best applied to which type of work?
C) Complex adaptive problems.

Scrum is most useful in the realm of creative, complex work. If the work is very well understood and repeatable, then a more simple resource-leveling pattern could be used. You wouldn't use the Scrum framework when washing your dishes after dinner, for example.

5. In Scrum, which role is responsible for assigning a new Team Member to a Team?
A) This is outside the scope of the Scrum framework.

The Scrum framework does not address hiring or adding Team Members to a Team. With that said, keep in mind that whenever the composition of the Team changes, you will be back in the Forming – Storming area of Bruce Tuckman's model. It is the Scrum Master's job to get the Team back to the Norming – Performing area as quickly as possible after Team membership changes.

6. What is the recommended maximum Sprint length?
B) one month or less

Two to four weeks is ideal, but the 'rules' say it can be as long as 31 days. Anything longer than a month increases risk and uncertainty. TH month was selected to correspond to an Organization's natural reporting cycle

7. What does the Agile Manifesto say about planning?
C) We value responding to change over following a plan.

The four values of the Agile Manifesto are written to value: x over y. In this case it is better to respond to change than continue to following a plan that no longer fits. Just because it is in the plan does not mean the plan becomes a forcing mechanism to make us do specific work. Especially, when complex work has large amounts of discovery and adaptation is required, change the plan.

8. When should the Sprint Burndown Chart be updated?
A) Not a formal Sprint Artifact

The Sprint Burndown graph was always a questionable graph because of its tendency to be misused and force work to done. Any tools that are used to measure and force work to done will cause Quality to decrease, this cannot be allowed. However, some people recommended The Sprint Burndown Chart should be updated daily once work for the day is complete.

9. What is the purpose of the Product Backlog?
B) For the Product Owner to collect Product Backlog Items (PBIs) for the product

The Product Backlog is where PBIs refined to be made ready for future Sprints. This is not to be confused with the Sprint Backlog Items (SBIs), which are the work Items for the current Sprint.

10. Which role is primarily responsible for making decisions of scope versus schedule?
A) The Product Owner

Scope versus schedule is a matter of Backlog Ordering. It is the

Product Owner that orders the backlog.

11. When does a Sprint end?
D) When the Sprint timebox expires.

Scrum is iterative, incremental, and timeboxed. When the Sprint timebox expires, the Sprint ends regardless of whether or not all the Stories are completed. The Sprint does not get extended and the Sprint does not restart.

12. Which role is primarily responsible for ensuring that the agreed upon process is followed?
B) The Scrum Master

Though the entire Team should follow the process, it is the Scrum Master that is responsible for maintaining the process and seeing that it is followed. Over time, as the Team matures, the Scrum Master role may become less pronounced as the Team takes ownership of its process.

13. Who guides the Team during a Sprint
A) The Team is self-organizing and product-focused.

Once the Sprint starts, the Team self---organizes and works with little to no outside guidance. The Product Owner should be available to answer questions as they arise, but does not tell the Team what to do.

14. Who attends the Sprint Planning meeting?
D) All of the above

It is during Sprint Planning that the Team selects the Stories for the Sprint. The Product Owner identifies the Stories in priority order, the Team pulls Stories into the Sprint, and the ScrumMaster facilitates as the need arises.

15. What is the purpose of the Sprint Review meeting?
C) For the Stakeholders to review the product and provide feedback.

The Product Owner should demonstrate the product for any Stakeholders that can provide meaningful feedback. The meeting should not be about the Stories accomplished in the Sprint per se; it should maintain a product focus – the main goal is feedback. If the Stakeholders are not providing feedback, then the Product Owner needs to find a way to engage them. This is your most important opportunity to find information that could make a better product. Don't squander it!

16. Which role is most likely to bring up impediments during the Daily Standup?
C) The Development Team

Impediments can be brought up by anyone, but Team Members are most likely to bring up impediments as they go about their daily activities.

17. Which role is responsible for maintaining the Product Backlog?
B) The Product Owner

The Product Backlog is the set of Stories for future Sprints. Although anyone can add Stories to the Product Backlog (or the Fridge in our metaphor), it is the Product Owner who maintains it to answer the question "what next?"

18. In a four week Sprint, how long should the Sprint Review meeting be?
B) At most 4 hours.

The Sprint Review is timeboxed at one hour per week of Sprint length: four hours for a four-week Sprint, two hours for a two-week Sprint, etc. In practice however, the length of the Sprint Review may be different. It is all about getting meaningful feedback. Four hours may be a good starting point, but the length may adjust as necessary to keep the Stakeholders engaged. If the Sprint length is shorter, the Sprint Review may take less time since there is feedback more often. What you do not want to happen is the Stakeholders dreading going to a Sprint Review because it lasts too long. If the meeting drags on, there is more chance of the Stakeholders mentally checking out and you losing out on valuable feedback. You may schedule it for four hours, but feel free to end it early if the meeting passes the point of usefulness.

19. What does the Agile Manifesto say about architecture?

C) The best architectures, requirements and designs emerge from self-organizing teams.

Obviously there may be architecture and infrastructure requirements up front, but architecture should emerge as the product grows. Just like there should not be big analysis upfront, there should not be big architecture upfront. Many times you will find grandiose generic architecture created that only ends up being used in one specific application. Work with reuse in mind, but don't over---architect simple solutions.

20. What does the Product Owner do during the Sprint?
B) Makes herself available to answer questions and provide clarifications.

The Product Owner should not interfere with the Team's daily activities; she should trust in the Team's ability to deliver. The Product Owner must be available to see that questions are answered in minutes and hours, not days and weeks.

21. What is a highly desirable quality of a good development team?
D) It is self-organizing.

The main power in Scrum is that of the self---organizing Team.

22. When should the progress towards goals be updated?
C) At least every Sprint.

The total work remaining each sprint can be summed and used to indicate progress towards the goals every sprint by the Product Owner. It should be updated after every Sprint to measure the releasable state of the product.

23. What are the three pillars that uphold the empirical process of Scrum?
C) Transparency, inspection, adaptation.

An empirical process is in contrast to a defined process. With a defined process, you must completely understand the system — given a well-defined set of inputs, you can expect the same set of outputs. Complex development efforts rarely lend themselves to a defined process, which is why Scrum is an empirical process. The two main components are frequent inspection and adaptation. The third component, transparency, emphasizes that the work must be kept visible so that it can be inspected and adapted.

24. Which role is responsible for the business value of the product delivered?
B) The Product Owner

The Product Owner is just that: the owner of the Product. She remains product---focused and works to increase the business value of the product.

25. Scrum has a definition of "Done", what does this help a Team produce?
B) An increment of potentially shippable product.

Everything deliverable the Team produces is an increment of "potentially shippable" product. The robust definition of Done helps the Team produce finished, potentially shippable product every Sprint.

Practice Exam #2

Choose the best answer to the following questions. The answers, as well as the rationale behind them, are provided after the exam

1. Once a Development Team commits to a Sprint Goal, what does the Team do?
   A. The Team performs whatever work is necessary to meet the Sprint Goal.
   B. The Team moves Stories from the Product Backlog to the Sprint Backlog.
   C. The Team performs tasks assigned by the Scrum Master.
   D. The Team determines the Done criteria for the Stories in the Sprint Backlog.

2. What does the Agile Manifesto say about customer collaboration?
   A. Let customers define the product with little input from other Stakeholders.
   B. The Development Team should solicit feedback from customers often.
   C. The Scrum Master is the only role that should interface with customers.
   D. Customers should only be involved once the product is nearing release.

3. What is the main purpose of the Sprint Backlog?
    A. For the Development Team to manage the work in the current Sprint.
    B. For the Product Owner to collect Stories for the product that may be done in later Sprints.
    C. For the Product Owner to manage the number of hours spent on the project.
    D. For the Scrum Master to measure progress of the current Sprint versus previous Sprints.

4. What is the main responsibility of the Product Owner role?
    A. Owning the process for the team.
    B. Guiding the Team's daily activities.
    C. Optimizing the value of the product.
    D. Balancing the power of the Scrum Master.

5. In Scrum what is the recommended length of Release Planning?
    A. 4 hours.
    B. 8 hours.
    C. ½ of 1 Sprint.
    D. Release planning is not a prescribed meeting in the Scrum Guide.

6. Which role facilitates the Sprint Retrospective meeting?
    A. The Scrum Master
    B. The Product Owner
    C. The Team self-facilitates
    D. The Business Owner

7. Once a Sprint has started, who determines how the Team works?
   A. The Scrum Master
   B. The Product Owner
   C. The Team
   D. The Business Owner

8. How does Scrum emphasize adapting to current conditions rather than following a plan?
   A. Changes can be made to the current Sprint whenever the Product Owner deems it necessary.
   B. Changes can be added to the Product Backlog at any time for possible inclusion in a Sprint.
   C. The Team prioritizes its own work for the next Sprint during Sprint Planning.
   D. Only the Product Owner can create Stories for the Product Backlog.

9. Which role creates releasable increment from the items in the Product Backlog?
   A. The Scrum Master
   B. The Product Owner
   C. The Development Team
   D. All of the above.

10. Can the Scrum Master and the Product Owner be the same person?
    A. Yes, as long as she has the time available to do both roles.
    B. Yes, as long as she is a Certified Scrum Master (CSM) and Certified Scrum Product Owner (CSPO).
    C. No, in order to fulfill regulatory compliance, they must be separate people.
    D. Yes, but it's risky as she would have too much power, and the roles are often driven by different motivations.

11. What does the Product Owner do during the Daily
    Standup?
    A. Introduces additional Stories for the current Sprint.
    B. The Product Owner's participation in the Daily Standup
        should be defined by the Development Team.
    C. Assigns Tasks to Team Members.
    D. Challenges and motivates the Team to reach the Sprint
        Goal.

12. What is the main responsibility of the Scrum Master
    role?
    A. Manage the Product Backlog.
    B. Own the Development Team's process and serve as the
        expert on Scrum.
    C. Assign Tasks to Team Members.
    D. Ensure that the product is meeting the Stakeholder's
        needs.

13. What does the Scrum framework say about
    planning?
    A. Plans are important, but adapting to current conditions
        is more important.
    B. Planning is unnecessary in Scrum.
    C. Planning should be done by Stakeholders external to
        the Scrum Team.
    D. Planning should be done before the first Sprint starts.

14. Who attends the Sprint Review meeting?
    A. Only the Product Owner and the Team.
    B. Only the Scrum Master and the Team.
    C. The Business Owner and the Product Owner.
    D. The Product Owner, Scrum Master, Team, and
        appropriate Stakeholders.

15. What is the main purpose of Sprint Planning?
    A. For the Product Owner to write Stories and Done criteria for the next Sprint.
    B. For the Product Owner to receive meaningful feedback from Stakeholders.
    C. For the Team to load the Sprint with Stories by "Agreement-driven planning"
    D. For the Scrum Master to adapt the process for the upcoming Sprint.

16. What does the Scrum Master do during the Sprint Retrospective?
    A. Seek meaningful feedback from the Stakeholders.
    B. Identify impediments for the current Sprint.
    C. Inform the Product Owner of the Tasks completed by each Team Member.
    D. Facilitate the improvement of the Team's process.

17. What is the purpose of the Product Vision?
    A. Provide detailed analysis of why the Team Members were chosen for the Team.
    B. Provide use cases for the product which the Team can break into actionable Stories.
    C. Provide a high-level view of the resulting product, and why it is valuable.
    D. Provide a description of the funding of the project.

18. What if a Team realizes it will not meet the Sprint Goal before the end of the Sprint?
    A. Work with the Product Owner to determine what can be delivered that will be valuable.
    B. Extend the Sprint length until something of value is produced.
    C. Abnormally terminate the Sprint and plan a new Sprint.
    D. Notify the Business Owner and ask for guidance.

19. What if the C.E.O. identifies crucial functionality in the middle of a Sprint?
    A. Add the Story to the current Sprint and work on it next.
    B. Add the Story to the next Sprint.
    C. Notify the Product Owner of the request so she can prioritize it in the Product Backlog.
    D. Abnormally terminate the Sprint and plan a new Sprint with the new Story in it.

20. What might happen if the Product Owner is unavailable during the Sprint?
    A. The product increment created during the Sprint may not satisfy business needs.
    B. The Scrum Master takes over the role of the Product Owner.
    C. The Sprint length is extended by one day for every day the Product Owner is absent.
    D. Abnormally terminate the Sprint and plan a new Sprint with a new Product Owner.

21. What if a Development Team Member raises an impediment during the Daily Standup?
    A. The Daily Standup does not end until the impediment is resolved.
    B. Development Team Members that are impacted by the impediment meet afterwards to discuss.
    C. The Product Owner extends the Sprint by one day.
    D. The impediment is noted and addressed during the Sprint Review.

22. What if the Product Owner has other responsibilities and is not available to the Development Team?
    A. Split the Product Owner role across two or more people.
    B. The Development Team should interface with the Business Owner directly to get questions answered.
    C. Remove the Product Owner's other responsibilities so she can focus on the Team and product.
    D. Reduce the number of Stories in the Sprint.

23. If a Team realizes it has committed to too much work for the Sprint, who should be involved with adjusting the Stories and Sprint Goal?
    A. The Product Owner
    B. The Scrum Master
    C. The Team
    D. All of the above.

24. How should the Scrum Master facilitate dialog between the Development Team and the Product Owner?
    A. Setup and facilitate meetings between the Product Owner and Development Team.
    B. Help the Team to talk in terms of business needs.
    C. Teach the Product Owner about the technologies used in the product.
    D. All of the above.

25. Which role is most concerned with removing impediments?
    A. The Product Owner
    B. The Scrum Master
    C. The Team
    D. The Business Owner

Practice Exam #2 (Answers)

Use this answer sheet to check your answers on the Practice Test.

1. Once a Team commits to a Sprint Goal, what does the Team do?

A) The Team performs whatever work is necessary to meet the Sprint Goal.

During each Sprint, the Team works to accomplish the Sprint Goal. The Team does want to complete all the Stories in a Sprint, but there should also be an elevating goal that answers the question "why were these Stories chosen?"

2. What does the Agile Manifesto say about customer collaboration?

B) The Development Team should solicit feedback from customers often.

Tight feedback loops are crucial to the success of a product. The sooner we can recognize adjustments to the product direction, the easier it is to adjust course.

3. What is the main purpose of the Sprint Backlog?

A) For the Team to manage the work in the current Sprint.

The Sprint Backlog (Front Burner) holds the work for the current Sprint. It provides a means for the Team to self---organize and also provides visibility of the work to those outside the Team.

4. What is the main responsibility of the Product Owner role?

C) Optimizing the value of the product.

The Product Owner is just that: the owner of the Product. She remains product---focused and works to increase the business value of the product.

5. In Scrum what is the recommended length of Release Planning?

D) Release planning is not a prescribed meeting in the Scrum Guide.

The Story is the fundamental unit of work in Scrum. A collection of Stories makes up a Sprint, and a collection of Sprints make up a Release. Release planning is important, but is not defined in Scrum.

6. Which role facilitates the Sprint Retrospective meeting?

A) The Scrum Master

The Scrum Master is the Team's Scrum expert and keeper of the process. The Scrum Master facilitates the Sprint Retrospective so that the Team can discover ways to improve the process.

7. Once a Sprint has started, who determines how the Development Team works?

C) The Team

Once the Sprint starts, the Team self-organizes and works with little to no outside guidance. The Product Owner should be available to answer questions as they arise, but should not does not tell the Team what to do.

8. How does Scrum emphasize adapting to current conditions rather than following a plan?
B) Changes can be added to the Product Backlog at any time for possible inclusion in a Sprint.

As new work is discovered, Stories are added to the Product Backlog (or the Fridge in our metaphor). If something of critical importance is discovered, it may need to be included in the current Sprint. This should be the exception and not the rule and it must be agreed to by the Team.

9. Which role creates releasable increment from the items in the Product Backlog?
B) The Development Team

It is the Development Team that turns Product Backlog Items into potentially releasable product increments. The Development Team pulls Product Backlog Items into the Sprint Backlog (at Sprint Planning) in the order determined by the Product Owner. The Development Team then creates the potentially releasable increment from the items in the Sprint Backlog.

10. Can the Scrum Master and the Product Owner be the same person?
D) Yes, but it's risky as she would have too much power, and the roles are often driven by different motivations.

The roles of the Scrum Master and the Product Owner are often at odds with each other. The Product Owner may attempt to drive the Team to complete the work on schedule, but it is the Scrum Master who must observe the system and determine if the Team is working at a sustainable pace. If these roles are held by the same person, then there are no checks and balances and the Team and product may suffer.

11. What does the Product Owner do during the Daily Standup?

B) The Product Owner's participation in the Daily Standup should be defined by the Development Team.

Scrum does not require the Product Owner to attend the Daily Standup, but it is in the interest of the Team and the product for the Product Owner to attend. The Product Owner can monitor progress and answer questions at the Daily Standup. Ultimately, the Team should decide if the Product Owner should attend the Daily Standup.

12. What is the main responsibility of the Scrum Master role?

B) Own the Team's process and serve as the expert on Scrum.

The Scrum Master should be an observer of the system, tuning the people and process drawing on expertise in Scrum for guidance. The Scrum Master facilitates wherever needed and places top priority on removing any impediments that arise. The Scrum Master should be a "people person," as she will be tuning a system of people.

13. What does the Scrum framework say about planning?

A) Plans are important, but adapting to current conditions is more important.

Planning is good and there should be some plan in place; however responding to current conditions is a far better guide for the work. The more work that is done on a project, the more domain knowledge is acquired, which leads to better decision making, rather than planning everything at the beginning of the project. "No plan survives first contact with the enemy." --- Moltke.

14. Who attends the Sprint Review meeting?
D) The Product Owner, Scrum Master, Team, and appropriate Stakeholders.

The Product Owner should demonstrate the product for any Stakeholders that can provide meaningful feedback. The Team and Scrum Master should be there to help the Product Owner engage the Stakeholders and assist as needed.

15. What is the main purpose of Sprint Planning?
C) For the Team to load the Sprint with Stories by "Agreement-driven planning."

Sprint Planning is where the work for the next Sprint is agreed upon. The Product Owner should have actionable Stories with complete Done criteria ready before going into Sprint Planning.

16. What does the Scrum Master do during the Sprint Retrospective?
D) Facilitate the improvement of the Team's process.

The Scrum Master is the Development Team's Scrum expert and keeper of the Scrum Framework. The Scrum Master facilitates the Sprint Retrospective so that the Team can discover ways to improve its process. It is important not to try to change too many things at once, maybe the top one or two things that are impacting the team the most.

17. What is the purpose of the Product Vision?
C) Provide a high-level view of the resulting product, and why it is valuable.

The Product Vision should not be a detailed view of the product. The details will inevitably change as the product matures. The Product Vision should describe why the product is worth building and provide a high-level end-state of the product. The Increment is a progressive step accomplished one sprint at a time until the goal is achieved.

18. What if a Team realizes it will not meet the Sprint Goal before the end of the Sprint?
A) Work with the Product Owner to determine what can be delivered that will be valuable.

There may be times that unforeseen circumstances cause the Sprint Goal to be in jeopardy. The important thing is to communicate this as early as possible to manage expectations. The Team, Product Owner, and Scrum Master should meet to see if there is something of value that can be delivered within the Sprint time-box.

19. What if the CEO identifies crucial functionality in the middle of a Sprint?
C) Notify the Product Owner of the request so she can prioritize it in the Product Backlog.

As new work is discovered, Stories are added to the Product Backlog (or the Fridge in our metaphor). If something of critical importance is discovered, it may need to be included in the current Sprint, but this needs to be a decision of the Product Owner and agreed to by the Team.

20. What might happen if the Product Owner is unavailable during the Sprint?

A) The product increment created during the Sprint may not satisfy business needs.

One of the major causes of failure of projects is the lack of a focused, rapidly responding Product Owner who can ensure that questions are answered in minutes and hours, not days and weeks. If the Product Owner is unavailable for much of a Sprint, the Team will still do the best that it can, but the product increment created will probably suffer. If the Product Owner continues to be unavailable during the Sprint, it may become an impediment to the team.

21. What if a Team Member raises an impediment during the Daily Standup?

B) Development Team members impacted by the impediment meet afterwards to discuss solutions.

The Daily Standup should be a short meeting, no more than 15 minutes. Any issues that are brought up during the Daily Standup should be noted and then addressed in break-out meetings with the necessary people. Do not waste the entire Team's time discussing issues that only affect certain Team Members.

22. What if the Product Owner has other responsibilities and is not available to the Development Team?

C) Remove the Product Owner's other responsibilities so she can focus on the Development Team and product.

One of the major causes of failure of projects is the lack of a focused, rapidly responding Product Owner who can ensure that questions are answered in minutes and hours, not days and weeks. If the Product Owner is split between the Team and other responsibilities, unless she has time for both, the product will suffer.

23. If a Team realizes it has committed to too much work for the Sprint, who should be involved with adjusting the Stories and Sprint Goal?
D) All of the above.

Especially with new Teams, there is a tendency to overestimate the amount of work that can be completed in a Sprint. As time goes on and the Team matures, the amount of work will normalize and become very consistent. In the event that the Team committed to too much, the Team, Product Owner, and Scrum Master should meet to see what can be completed that will provide the most business value. This may mean moving Stories out of the current Sprint or adjusting the Done criteria of the Stories (and creating new Stories to capture the removed portion of the Done criteria).

24. How should the Scrum Master facilitate dialog between the Product Owner Development Team?
D) All of the above.

The Scrum Master has many tools at her disposal for facilitating dialog between different parties. Normally the Team Members are more technically skilled than the Product Owner, so it helps if the Team Members talk more in terms of business needs and ideas. Also the Product Owner can learn about some of the technical details of the product, at least at a high level.

25. Which role is most concerned with removing impediments?

B) The Scrum Master

The Scrum Master facilitates the Team's work and removing impediments is crucial. This is not to say that the Scrum Master should actually solve every impediment – she may not have the domain knowledge necessary to do so, but she should work to ensure that every impediment is removed.

References

Exploring Scrum: The Fundamentals, 2d Edition,
https://exploringscrum.com
This is a book on "modern Scrum" that focuses almost entirely on what works and what has not worked from a practitioner's point of view. It has been written as a reference book and is currently being updated to a 2nd edition.

Scrum Guide, https://www.scrumguide.com/

The Scrum Guidebook: Analysis of the 2017 Scrum Guide has been written to help students decipher the numerous updates made to the Scrum Guide. Ken and Jeff have updated it numerous times to reflect their changes and view on Scrum. An annotated version is available that can be used to help a student build a consistent understanding.

Scrum Dictionary, https://scrumdictionary.com

The Scrum Dictionary provides a stabilized set of terms that will help students, organizations or just about anyone have a more coherent understanding. For example, 'Scrum-Agile' or 'Agile-Scrum' are usually indicators that the concept is one big mess so both words are crammed together to cover 'it all'. The Scrum dictionary can help you pick through the mess and gain clarity.

Agile Manifesto, http://agilemanifesto.org
The Agile Manifesto is brilliant for its focus on agile and helping focus the public sector on the importance of agility in modern project work, especially software.

51891163R00062

Made in the USA
Middletown, DE
06 July 2019